M000316743

Amazing
Theme-Based
ESL Worksheets for Beginners

THEME: FOOD

Baye Hunter

© 2013 by Baye Hunter, Hunter Publishing, Toronto, Canada.

All rights reserved. Teachers may make copies for classroom use only. Otherwise no part of this book may be reproduced or transmitted in any form or by any means, electronic or mechanical, including photocopying, recording, scanning, photographing, or by any information storage and retrieval system without permission in advance in writing from the author.

Thank you to www.clker.com for use of domain free clipart.

First edition.

ISBN: 978-0-9917641-3-6
Hunter Publishing

ABOUT THE AUTHOR

Baye Hunter has been a teacher of adult ESL at the Toronto District School Board since 1988. She has taught all levels. She holds a Bachelor of Education, Bachelor of Arts and a TESL Certificate. She has also taught in Hong Kong and Australia. She co-won with Ann Marie Guy the grand prize at the TESL Ontario Conference for her video "Let's All Go to the AGO" (on youtube). Visit her website at www.bayehunter.com for free downloadable activities.

ABOUT THE BOOK

Amazing Theme-Based ESL Worksheets for Beginners is based on vocabulary for the development of language foundations and on the premise that ESL learners must use a word several times in context to be able to remember it. Reading, writing, listening, speaking, grammar and communicative activities are built around the vocabulary. The book has a series of flash cards. These images may be used in various lessons, to introduce and reinforce the vocabulary and language structures.

 Hunter Publishing

Table of Contents

Food Vocabulary 1

Match the words to the pictures:

carrot	bread	corn	chicken	hot dog	pear
apple	coffee	potatoes	ice cream	cheese	muffin
eggs	milk	banana	steak	strawberries	spaghetti
fish	watermelon	cake	hamburger	beans	rice
		tomato			

1.	2.	3.	4.	5.

6.	7.	8.	9.	10.

11.	12.	13.	14.	15.

16.	17.	18.	19.	20.

21.	22.	23.	24.	25.

Food Vocabulary 2

Match the words to the pictures:

cucumber	avocado	sandwich	cherries	sugar	sushi
apple juice	wine	kiwi	hamburger	cauliflower	soup
tea	peach	broccoli	pancakes	grapefruit	pumpkin
pepper	eggplant	French fries	grapes	cabbage	garlic

1.	2.	3.	4.	5.

6.	7.	8.	9.	10.

11.	12.	13.	14.	15.

16.	17.	18.	19.	20.

21.	22.	23.	24.

Food Vocabulary - Listening

Listen to your teacher say the words. Write **i** or **ee** under the pictures.

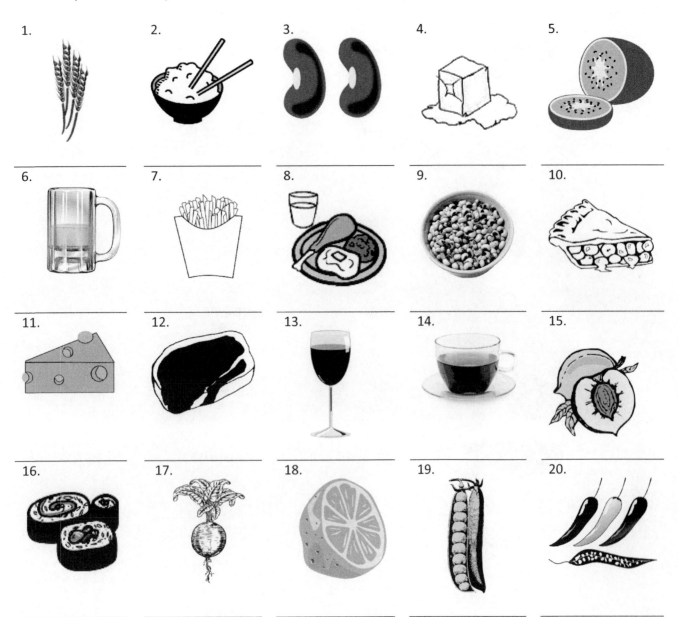

1.

2.

3.

4.

5.

6.

7.

8.

9.

10.

11.

12.

13.

14.

15.

16.

17.

18.

19.

20.

Words

1. wheat 2. rice 3. beans 4. ice 5. kiwi 6. beer 7. fries 8. meal 9. beans 10. pie 11. cheese
12. meat 13. wine 14. tea 15. peach 16. su**shi** 17. beet 18. lime 19. peas 20. chi**li**

Which word is the correct spelling?

		A	B	C
1.		appel	apple	aplle
2.		beer	bear	bere
3.		cherrie	chery	cherry
4.		pear	peer	pere
5.		steek	steak	stake
6.		eggplant	egplant	eggpatnl
7.		hamberger	hambergur	hamburger
8.		flore	flower	flour
9.		cucummer	cukummer	cucumber
10.		cheese	chess	chose

8

Food Vocabulary 2 - Crossword

Across

2.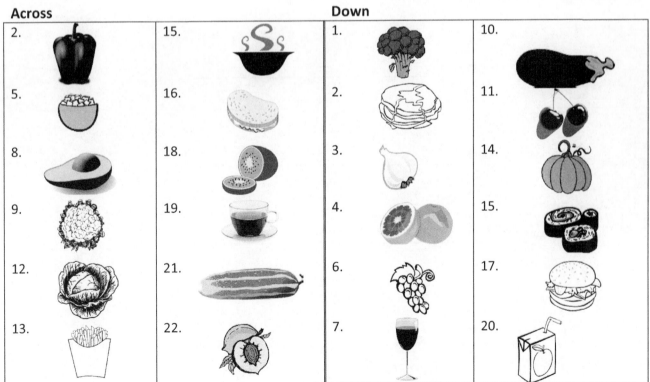
5.
8.
9.
12.
13.
15.
16.
18.
19.
21.
22.

Down

1.
2.
3.
4.
6.
7.
10.
11.
14.
15.
17.
20.

Shopping for Food: How much is / are...?

Write **is** or **are** and the food word:

$2.99

1. How much <u>is</u> <u>the watermelon</u>?

2. How much_____?

3. How much_____?

4. How much_____?

5. How much_____?

6. How much_____?

7. How much_____?

8. How much_____?

| strawberries | kiwi | watermelon | salt and pepper |
| cherries | coffee | sugar | walnuts |

9.   How much_____?

10.   How much_____?

11.   How much_____?

12.   How much_____?

13.   How much_____?

14.   How much_____?

15.   How much_____?

16.   How much_____?

milk	rice	corn	apples
carrots	ice cream	chicken	olive oil

Countable and uncountable nouns

Are these nouns countable or uncountable? Use a dictionary.

1. flour _____

2. cream _____

3. coconut _____

4. bread _____

5. apple _____

6. meat _____

7. celery _____

8. snack_____

9. tea _____

10. asparagus _____

11. milk_____

12. honey_____

13. cheese_____

14. banana_____

15. pasta_____

16. water _____

17. fruit _____

18. walnut_____

19. oil _____

20. potato_____

21. blueberry_____

22. yogurt_____

23. wheat_____

24. tomato _____

25. food _____

26. chocolate _____

27. avocado _____

28. steak_____

29. hamburger_____

30. hot dog_____

In the Kitchen: How much or how many?

How many + countable noun > How many apples **are** there?

How much + uncountable noun > How much milk **is** there?

Make sentences about the following:

1. How _much apple juice is there_ in the kitchen_?

2. How_____?

3. How_____?

4. How_____?

5. How_____?

6. How_____?

| bread | mushrooms | eggs | soup | muffins | apple juice |

7. How_____?

8. How_____?

9. How_____?

10. How_____?

11. How_____?

12. How_____?

13. How_____?

| rice | cherries | potatoes | beer |
| flour | | oil | pears |

14

What's on the table?

There is a/an + countable singular	
There is some + non-countable	There are some + countable plural

List the items on the table. Use <u>there is a/an</u> / <u>there is some</u> / <u>there are some</u>.

1. *There is a banana on the table.*

2. _____

3. _____

4. _____

5. _____

6. _____

7. _____

8. _____

Ordering Food in a Restaurant

Waiter: Would you like something to eat or drink?

Customer: Yes, I would like <u>some soup, some fish, and some coffee.</u>

Waiter: Anything else?

Customer: Yes, some <u>ice cream</u> for dessert.

Practise the dialogue with your neighbour.

Food – Adjective Match

Match 3 of the following adjectives with each of the food below. Some adjectives can be used more than once.

sweet	soft	creamy	delicious	spicy	small
hot	colourful	sour	long	green	greasy
purple	salty	healthy	unhealthy	yucky	purple
colourful	cold	convenient	red	hard	crunchy

1. _____

2. _____

3. _____

4. _____

5. _____

6. _____

7. _____

8. _____

9. _____

10. _____

11. _____

12. _____

Food Adjectives - Opposites

Match the words that mean the opposite:

A.

1. black _white_	7. good _____
2. bright _____	8. hard _____
3. cold _____	9. wet _____
4. cool _____	10. hot _____
5. dark _____	11. big _____
6. fat _____	12. interesting _____

white	soft	bad	hot	dry	boring
warm	dull	thin	cold	light	small

B.

1. long _____	7. smooth _____
2. ripe _____	8. healthy _____
3. open _____	9. sweet _____
4. beautiful _____	10. crunchy _____
5. strong _____	11. raw _____
6. delicious _____	12. stale _____

rough	short	sour	unripe	yucky	cooked
ugly	unhealthy	closed	weak	fresh	creamy

Food Adjectives Crossword - Opposites

Put the word that means the opposite:

Across

1. unripe
6. dry
7. yucky
10. smooth
11. cold
12. short
13. closed
14. crunchy

Down

2. boring
3. stale
4. sour
5. bad
8. unhealthy
9. fat
15. cooked

Food – Comparative Adjectives

one syllable words	2 syllable ending in -y	2 or more syllables
adjective + -er	adjective + -ier	more + adjective
small > smaller than	yummy > yummier than	beautiful > more beautiful than

Use the adjectives to make comparative sentences about the animals:

sweet	soft	creamy	delicious	spicy	small
round	colourful	sour	long	green	big
purple	salty	healthy	unhealthy	yucky	purple
colourful	expensive	cheap	red	hard	crunchy
hot	cold	convenient	necessary	common	greasy

1. An apple is **sweeter than** a carrot.

2.

3.

4.

5.

6.

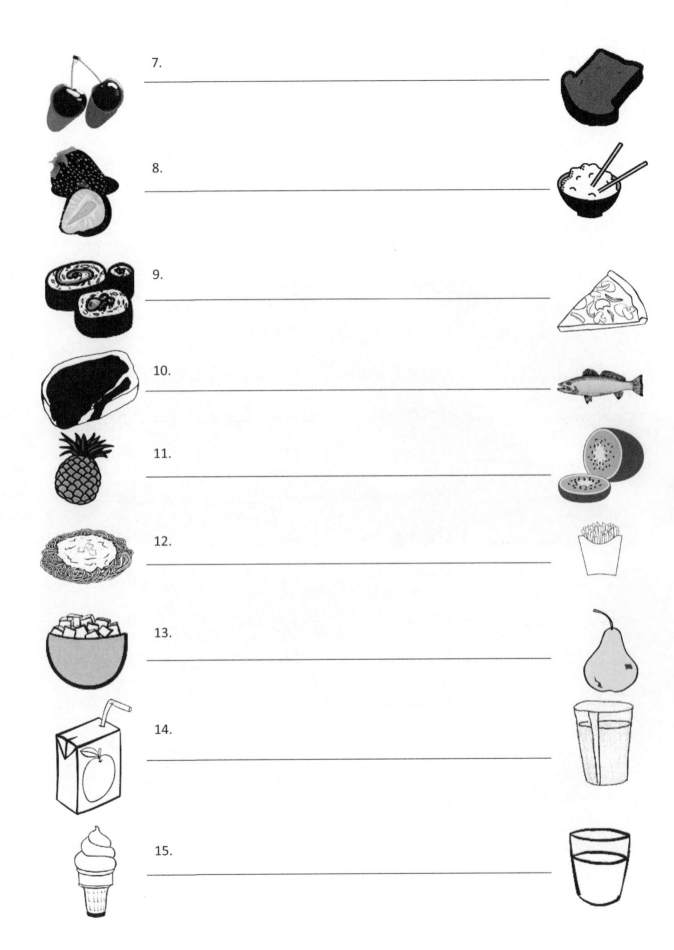

7. _____

8. _____

9. _____

10. _____

11. _____

12. _____

13. _____

14. _____

15. _____

A or An?

an + vowel sound (a e i o u) example: **an almond**

a + consonant sound (b c d f g h j k l m n p q r s t v w x y z) example: **a pear**

Put an 'a' or 'an' before the words:

1. _____oatmeal cookie

2. _____herb

3. _____ banana

4. _____ udon noodle

5. _____ olive

6. _____ dessert

7. _____ English muffin

8. _____ cherry

9. _____ beet

10. _____ octopus

11. _____ hot dog

12. _____ eggplant

13. _____squash

14. _____apricot

15. _____radish

16. _____trout

17. _____dumpling

18. _____oyster

19. _____pea

20. _____haddock

21. _____eel

22. _____orange

23. _____pickle

24. _____ice cream

25. _____zucchini

26. _____bok choy

Food Colours

Put the following foods into the colour groups below:

tomatoes	potatoes	eggplant	orange	lemon
lime	carrot	strawberries	grapefruit	cherries
blueberries	blackberries	chicken	milk	beef
lettuce	bok choy	zucchini	oyster	salmon
banana	noodles	rice	mushrooms	eggs
kiwi	sugar	watermelon	salt	pepper
coffee	corn	beets	cream	cucumber

red	orange	purple

yellow	white	blue

pink	brown	green

Which word doesn't belong?

Circle the word that is different in each row:

1. apple   orange   spinach   banana

2. chicken   beef   turkey   duck

3. juice   milk   yoghurt   cream

4. orange   lime   asparagus   grapefruit

5. spinach   beets   celery   lettuce

6. coffee   sugar   salt   pepper

7. zucchini   cucumber   tomato   pickle

8. eel   trout   salmon   pork

9. cherry   apple   strawberry   peach

10. pea   almond   peanut   cashew

11. honey   wheat   sugar   maple syrup

12. pumpkin   carrot   sweet potato   eggplant

A, An or Some?

a/an + singular nouns	example: a carrot / an egg
some + plural nouns	example: some carrots
some + non-count nouns	example: some water

Put a / an / some in the following sentences:

1. Mary is eating _____some_____carrots.

2. Ana is drinking _____tea.

3. Paul is chewing on _____gum.

5. Antonio is buying _____broccoli.

7. Hong has _____apples in his bag.

8. There are _____potatoes in the fridge.

9. Would you like _____orange?

10. There is _____milk in the fridge.

11. We need _____ice cream.

12. Can I have _____strawberry?

13. Can you buy_____avocados at the store?

14. Would you like _____sugar in your coffee?

How often?

always
usually
sometimes
never

Talk about yourself. How often do you eat or drink these things? Use the words above. Use the verb 'drink' or 'eat.' Tell your neighbour.

1.   I _never_ _eat_ broccoli.

2.   I _____ _drink_ tea.

3.   I _____ _____ chocolate.

4.   I _____ _____ beer.

5.   I _____ _____ carrots.

6.   I _____ _____ rice.

7.   I _____ _____ chicken.

8.   I _____ _____ avocado.

9.   I _____ _____ cabbage.

10. I _____ _____ wine.

11. I _____ _____ cucumbers.

12. I _____ _____ apple juice.

Healthy or Unhealthy?

coffee

broccoli

ice cream

grapefruit

olive oil

chocolate

hamburger

muffins

beer

sushi

sugar

pizza

milk

cake

cabbage

hot dog

French fries

bread

cheese

potatoes

Put the words in the box below:

Healthy Foods	Unhealthy Foods

Nutrition

Work in small groups with picture dictionaries. Find 2-3 foods with these qualities:

Good for bones and teeth (calcium)	Helps to fight colds (vitamins)	Gives you energy (protein)	Good for digestion (fiber)	Bad for you

Contains caffeine	Good for your skin	High in fat	Good for your eyes	High in sugar

Food Adjectives

Using a picture dictionary, name three foods for each category.

round	sweet	sour	long	small	big

colourful	soft	green	red	hard	crunchy

spicy	hot	cold	bland	creamy	delicious

purple	crumbly	healthy	unhealthy	yucky	bakeable

Food - Bingo Cards

Foods - Flashcards

Practise the following phrases with the flash cards with the learners:

1. Write one of the phrases on the board, show the students the pictures one at a time and the learners must say the phrase with the word.

    I like/I don't like _____?

    Do you like _____? Yes, I do. No I don't.

    Would you like some_____?

    We need some more_____. We are out of _____.

    Could you please pass the_____?

    Do you have a/some_____?

    May I borrow your _____?

    Where is the _____?

    Do you know where the _____ is?

    Practise the prepositions in, on, under, beside/next to, over , and in using two images at a time and asking – Where is the_____?

    Where can I buy some _____?

    How much is/are the _____?

    The _____ costs $29.95. (Do this as a dictation for practising prices)

    How many _____ do you have?

2. Make a grid across the board with A B and C across the top. Put three pictures across under each letter. Add several rows to this and do a dictation either with single words, full sentences or questions.

3. Have students work in groups of 2-3. Give each group a sheet of paper and a small set of food flashcards. Have them write a recipe using the foods in the pictures. Have them present to the class, writing the recipe on the board.

33

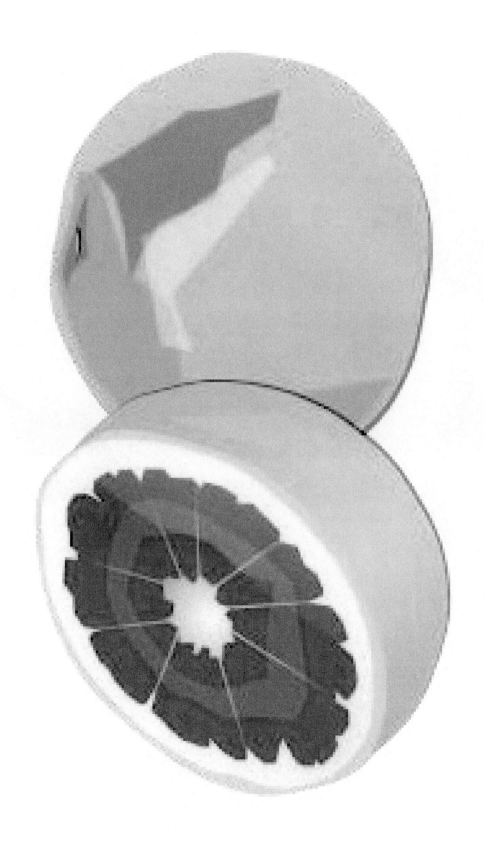

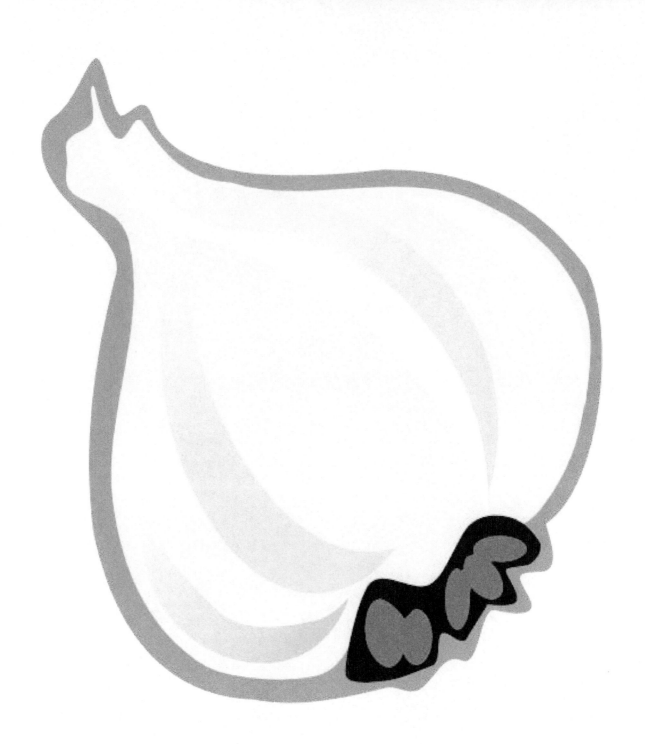

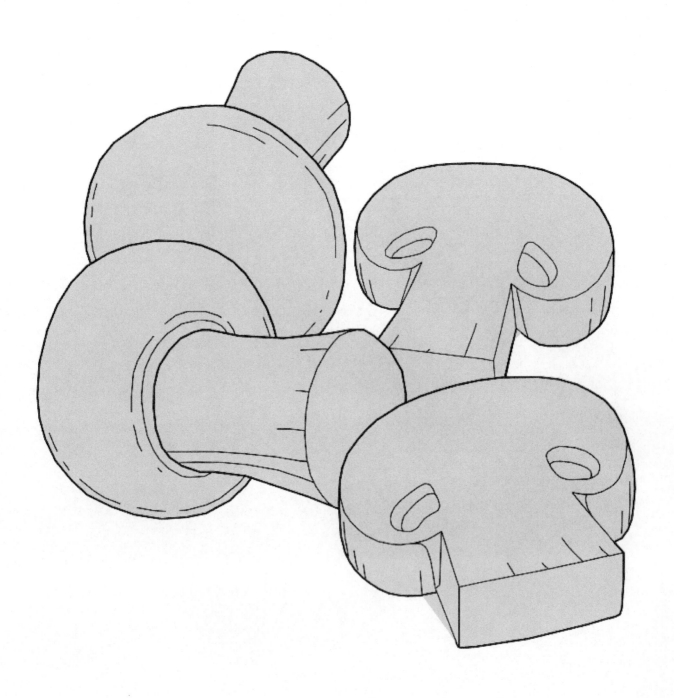

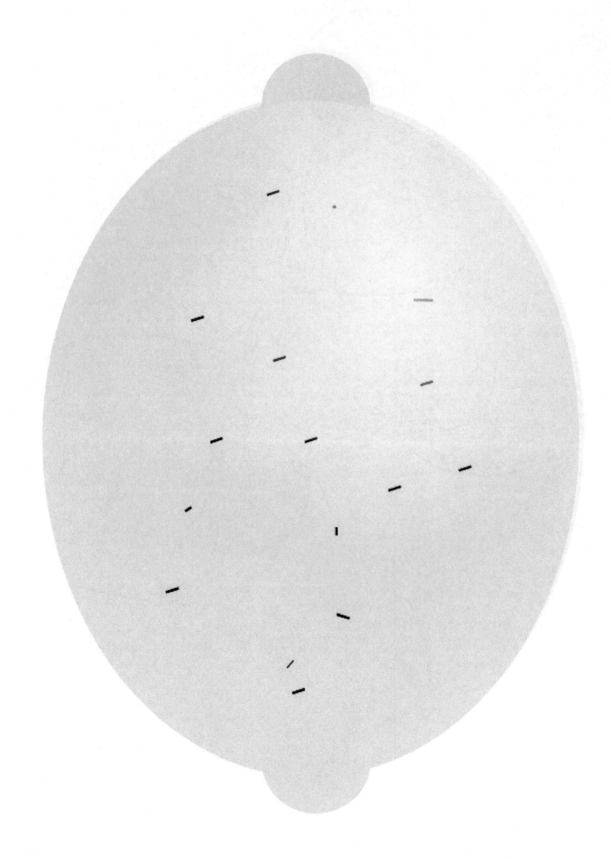

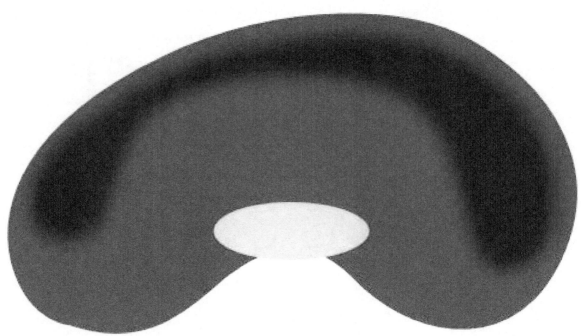

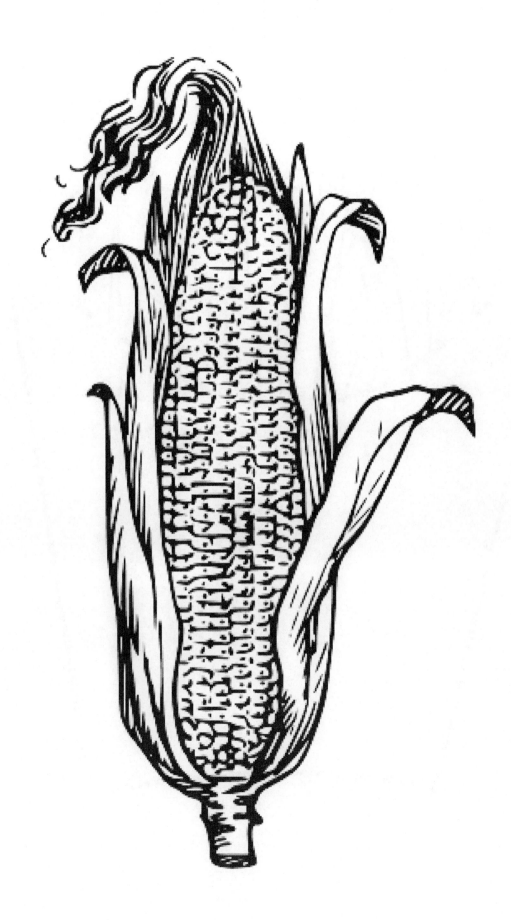

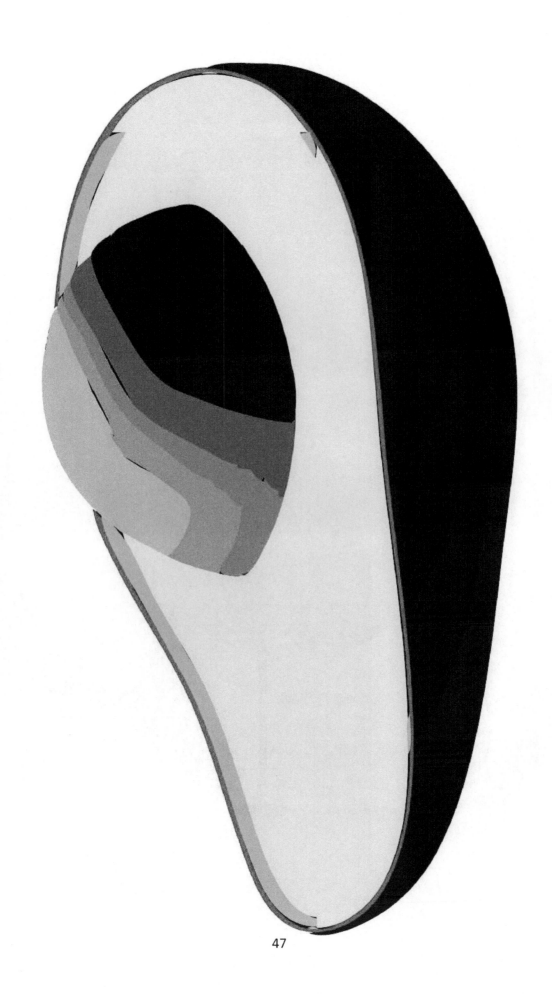

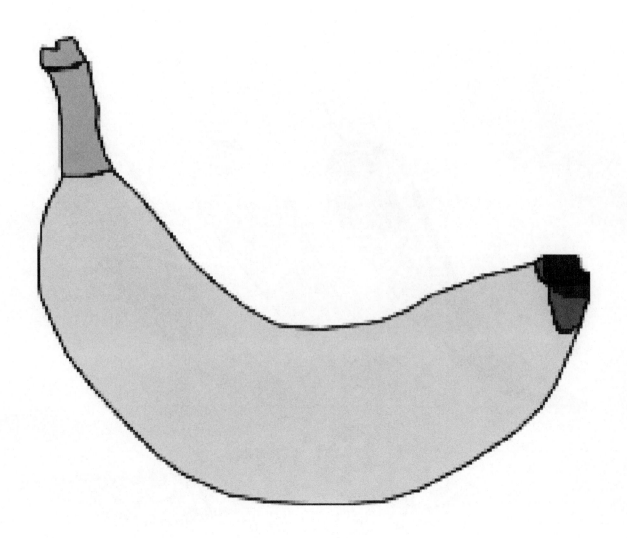

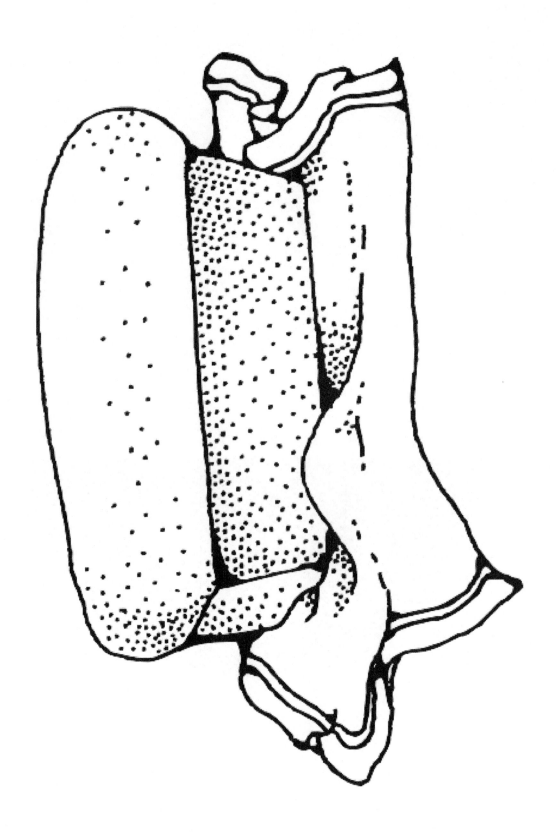

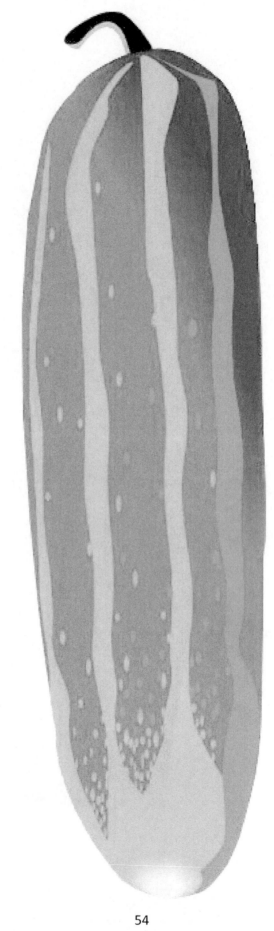

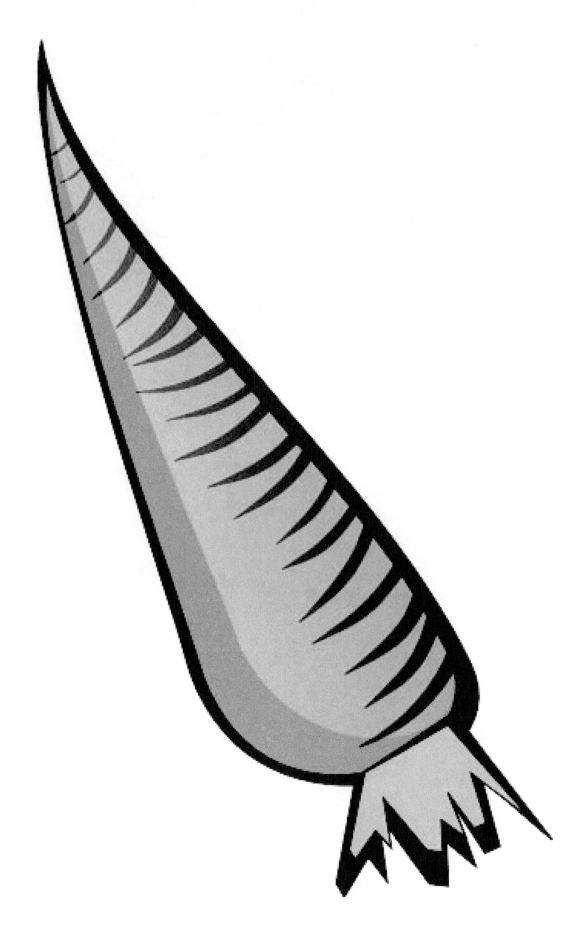

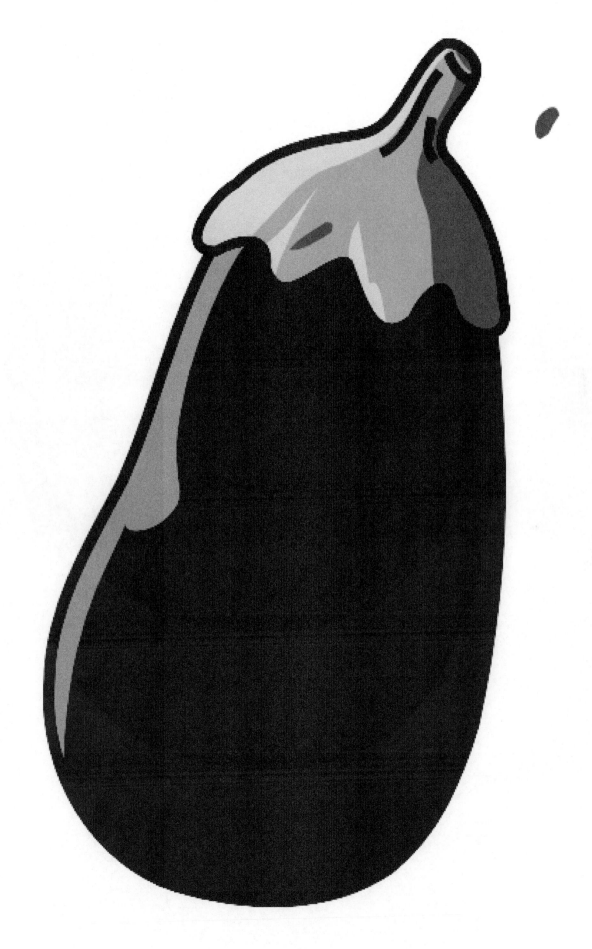

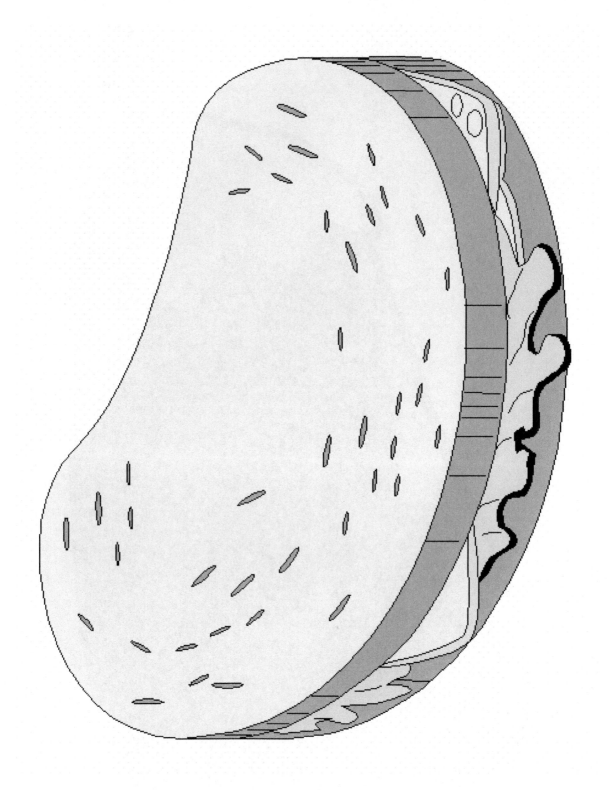

64

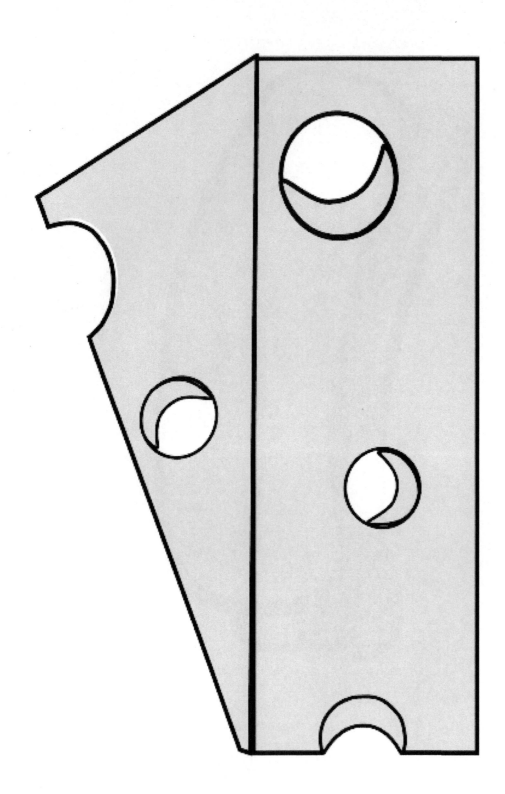

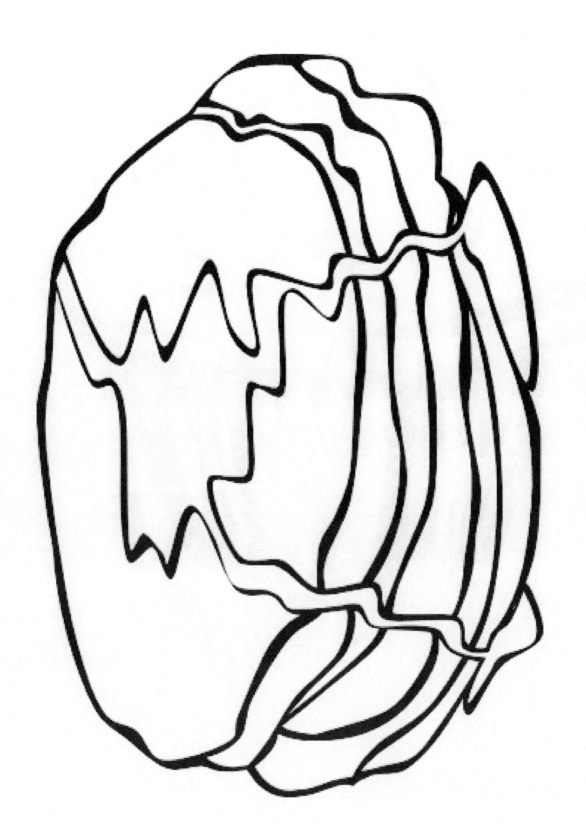

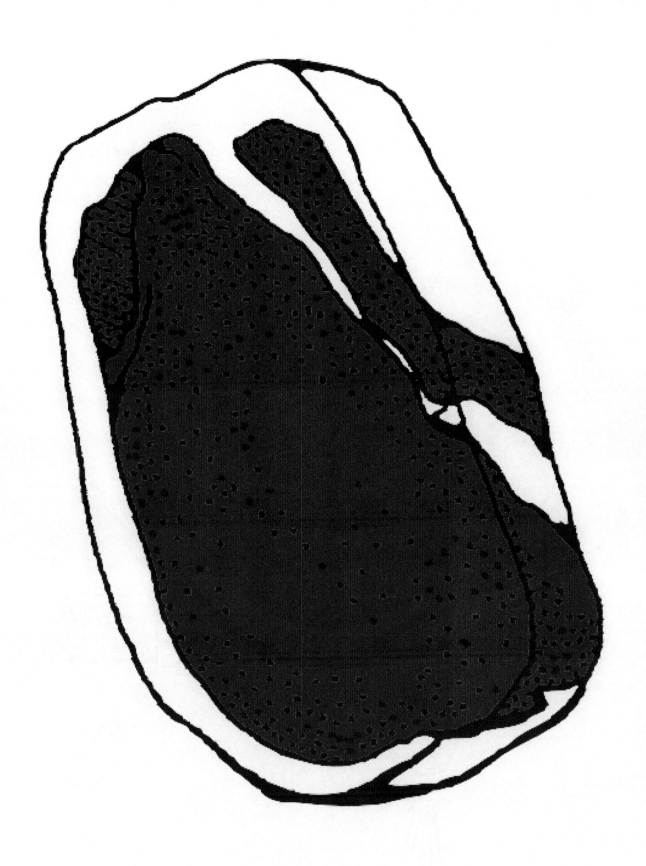

Kitchen Tools 1 Vocabulary

toaster	can opener	bowl	colander	blender	measuring spoons
fork	knife	microwave	teapot	napkin	salt shaker

1. _____

2. _____

3. _____

4. _____

5. _____

6. _____

7. _____

8. _____

9. _____

10. _____

11. _____

12. _____

Kitchen Tools 1 Crossword

Across

5.

8.

9.

10.

11.

Down

1.

2.

3.

4.

5.

6.

7.

Kitchen Tools 1 - Word Search

```
P M T K H F N F B E P D S C D
T W I O S R O T R X K H N O T
V F E C P M O R T H X W O L I
U X G W R A E D K W M J O A S
B O W L S O E B O O C F P N K
C K V T H N W T Z P P R S D C
H B E F G W J A K R E U G E F
P R E D N E L B V K K B N R D
Q D S B H W Q D A E X Y I A N
I Z Y X G L C H V L F N R B O
Q K J E E K S Q I P K I U H T
H S I F Z T A S Z G U K S Y A
I E I F L D G T I M O P A A K
T N C A N O P E N E R A E I G
K G S C C U E R M S T N M G F
```

Kitchen Words 1 - Scramble

Unscramble each of the clue words.

Copy the letters in the numbered cells to other cells with the same number.

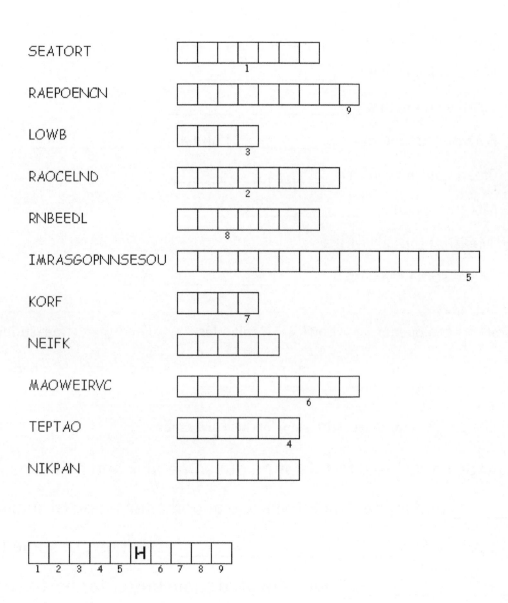

SEATORT

RAEPOENCN

LOWB

RAOCELND

RNBEEDL

IMRASGOPNNSESOU

KORF

NEIFK

MAOWEIRVC

TEPTAO

NIKPAN

Kitchen Tools 1 - Sentences

A. Complete the sentences

1. Make some toast with a _____.

2. Heat your food in a_____.

3. Rinse the pasta with a_____.

4. Mix a milkshake with a_____.

5. Open a can with a_____.

6. Eat your food with a_____and a _____.

7. Clean your face with a _____.

8. Mix the recipe in a_____.

9. Measure the salt with a _____.

10. Make some tea with a_____.

toaster	can opener	bowl	colander	blender	measuring spoon
fork	knife	microwave	teapot	napkin	

B. Complete the sentences with some of the words above:

Paul made some breakfast. First he put some milk and a banana in a ___

_____ and made a milkshake. He added a teaspoon of sugar to the

milkshake with a _____. Then he put some bread in

the _____. Then he heated some butter for his toast in the_

_____. He ate his toast with a _____and a _____

_____. He put some cereal in a_____and ate it. He put hot

water and a tea bag tea in the_____. He wiped his face with a _

_____.

76

Kitchen Tools 1 - Listening

Listen and choose the right word:

Kitchen Tools 1 - Verb Matching

Match the tool with the verb:

1.

2.

3.

4.

5.

6.

7.

8.

9.

10.

a. heat

b. measure

c. strain

d. toast

e. cut

f. sprinkle

g. open

h. hold

i. blend

j. wipe

Kitchen Tools 1 - Present Continuous

I am + verb + -ing	I **am baking** bread.
She is + verb + -ing	She **is cooking** chicken.
They are + verb + -ing	They **are steaming** broccoli.

What are they doing? Use the verbs at the bottom.

1. He_____*is toasting*_____ bread.

2. She _____ a can of soup.

3. He_____salt on the soup.

4. I _____some coffee.

5. We _____some flour.

| heat | toast | measure | sprinkle | open |

6. He_____the lettuce.

7. They _____a milkshake.

8. She_____her face.

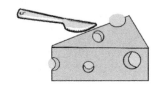

9. I _____cheese.

10. She_____some tea.

| cut | pour | wipe | rinse | blend |

80

Kitchen Tools 1 - Simple Past

I + verb + -ed	Last weekend I **baked** bread.
She + verb + -ed	Yesterday she **cooked** chicken.
They + verb + -ed	Last week they **steamed** broccoli.

What did they do? Use the verbs at the bottom. Put them in the past tense.

1. He____*toasted*____ bread.

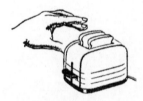

2. She _____ a can of soup.

3. He_____salt on the soup.

4. I _____some coffee.

5. We _____some flour.

heat	toast	measure	sprinkle	open

6. He_____the lettuce.

7. They _____a milkshake.

8. She_____her face.

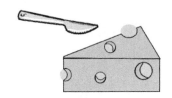

9. I _____cheese.

10. She_____some tea.

| cut* | pour | wipe | rinse | blend |

* irregular past tense = cut

Kitchen Tools 1 - Verbs - Crossword

Across

4.

7.

9.

10.

Down

1.

2.

3.

5.

6.

8.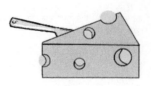

Kitchen Tools 2 - Vocabulary

| lid | steamer | pot | rolling pin | spoon | cutting board |
| apron | sauce pan | spatula | cheese slicer | knives | baking loaf pan |

1. _____

2. _____

3. _____

4. _____

5. _____

6. _____

7. _____

8. _____

9. _____

10. _____

11. _____

12. _____

Kitchen Tools 2 - Listening

Listen and circle the right picture:

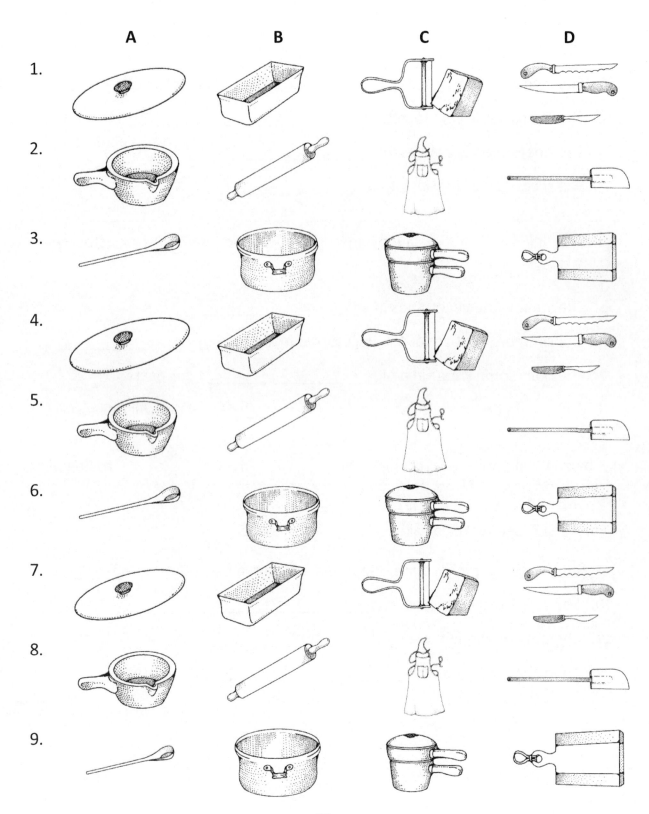

	A	B	C	D
1.				
2.				
3.				
4.				
5.				
6.				
7.				
8.				
9.				

Susie Makes Some Lunch

cutting board	apron	cheese slicer	colander

Susie makes lunch.

1. First she wears an_____ to keep her clothes clean.

2. She chops some vegetables with a _____ and a knife.

3. She rinses the vegetables in a _____.

4. She slices some cheese with a _____.

lid	sauce pan	pot	steamer

5. She steams the vegetables in a _____.

6. She simmers a sauce for the vegetables in a _____.

7. She boils some water in a big _____for pasta.

8. She covers the pot with a _____so it will boil faster.

baking loaf pan	mixing bowl	oven	rolling pin

For dessert she makes a cake.

9. She mixes flour, chocolate, sugar and water in a big _____.

10. She spreads the dough with a _____.

11. She puts the dough in a _____.

12. Then she bakes it in the _____ for 20 minutes.

Kitchen Tools 2 - Verb Matching

Match the tool with the verb:

 1.   a. steam

 2.   b. cover

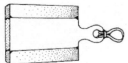 3.   c. bake

 4.   d. simmer

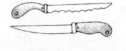 5.   e. stir

 6.   f. wear

 7.   g. slice

 8.   h. spread

 9.   i. chop

 10.   j. cut

Kitchen Verbs - Crossword

Across

2.

6.

3.

7.

4.

Down

1.

5.

3.

7.

4.

Kitchen Verbs - Simple Past

I + verb + -ed	Last weekend I **baked** bread.
She + verb + -ed	Yesterday she **cooked** chicken.
They + verb + -ed	Last month they **rinsed the** broccoli.

What did they do? Use the verbs at the bottom. Put them in the past tense.

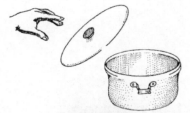
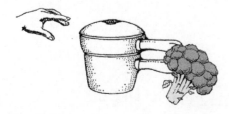

1. She _____ the broccoli.

2. He _____ the pot with the lid.

3. They _____ the muffins.

4. Mary _____ a sauce for the chicken.

5. The chef _____ the soup.

| stir | bake | cover | steam | simmer |

6. Nancy _____ the flour, milk, eggs and oil together.

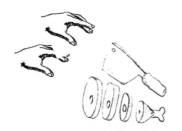

7. They _____ the meat.

8. John_____ the bread.

9. I_____the potatoes.

10. Susan_____the dishes.

| mix | slice | boil | chop | wash |

Kitchen Tools 2 - Crossword

Across

2.

4.

5.

6.

8.

9.

10.

11.

Down

1.

2.

3.

7.

Kitchen Tools 3 - Vocabulary

plate	dishwasher	wok	potato peeler
measuring cup	chopsticks	bottle opener	salt and pepper shakers
kettle	fridge	paper towels	frying pan

1. _____

2. _____

3. _____

4. _____

5. _____

6. _____

7. _____

8. _____

9. _____

10. _____

11. _____

12. _____

Kitchen Tools – Making Questions

Is this a _____?

Are these_____s?

1. _____

2. _____

3. _____

4. _____

5. _____

6. _____

7. _____

8. _____

9. _____

10. _____

11. _____

12. _____

13. _____

14. _____

15. _____

16. _____

17, _____

18. _____

Kitchen Verbs – Past Tense

Put the following verbs into the past tense and then the 3 different pronunciation groups:

cook	mix	slice	chop	wash
stir	steam	cover	simmer	pour
wipe	rinse	heat	measure	sprinkle
open	wipe	toast	heat	boil
wash	grate	broil	burn	melt
melt	refrigerate	cool	rub	roast
fry	sift	weigh	mash	knead

Voiceless	Voiced	After t or d
pronounced as 't' as in 'baked' f, k, p, s, ch, sh	pronounced as 'd' as in 'simmered' b, g, j, l, m, n, r, th, v, z, vowels	pronounced as 'id' as in 'blended' (add a syllable)

Kitchen Tools - Prepositions

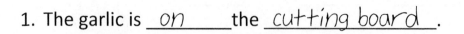

~~on~~	in	behind
next to	under	in front of

Put the prepositions and names of kitchen tools in the following sentences:

1. The garlic is ___on___ the _cutting board_ .

2. The milk is _____ the _____ .

3. The bread is _____ the _____ .

4. The spatula is _____ the frying pan.

5. The olive oil is_____ the _____ .

6. The cheese slicer is_____ the _____ .

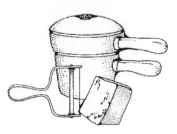

Kitchen Tools - Prepositions

| behind | in | in front of |
| next to | under | on top of |

Put the prepositions and names of kitchen tools in the following sentences:

1. The salt is _____ the _____.

2. The bottle opener is _____ the _____ .

3. The blender is _____ the _____*teapot*_____ .

4. The kettle is _____ the_____ .

5. The coffee is_____ the _____ .

6. The chopsticks are_____ the _____ .

Kitchen Tools 3 - Listening

Your teacher will call out one of the words and you must circle the correct one out of the three. To make it harder she may say the word in a sentence.

A   B   C

1.

2.

3.

4.

5.

6.

7.

7.

8.

9.

10.

11.

12.

13.

14.

15.

Prices Dictation

Listen to the dictation and write down the prices:

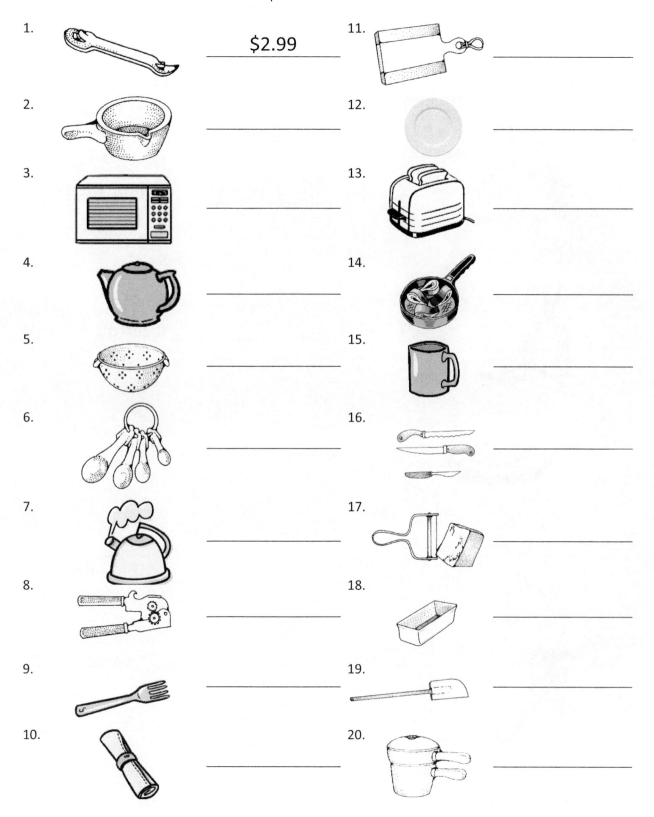

1. $2.99

2.

3.

4.

5.

6.

7.

8.

9.

10.

11.

12.

13.

14.

15.

16.

17.

18.

19.

20.

Kitchen Tools Review - Present Continuous

I am + verb + -ing	I **am baking** bread.
She is + verb + -ing	She **is cooking** chicken.
They are + verb + -ing	They **are steaming** broccoli.

What are they doing? Use the verbs at the bottom.

1. She_____*is baking*_____some bread.

2. He _____ a carrot.

3. He_____vegetables.

4. I _____some flour.

5. We _____some bread.

| ~~bake~~ | chop | measure | slice | fry |

6. She_____the ingredients.

7. They _____some bread.

8. She_____some salt.

9. I _____a pancake.

10. She_____some tea.

| flip | mix | wipe | toast | pour |

Recipes

Put the instructions for the following recipes in the correct order:

How to make Basmati rice

Ingredients:

1. 1 cup white Basmati rice
2. 2 cups water

Instructions:

_____ Put the pot on the stove top on high heat.

_____ First, rinse the rice in cold water.

_____ Bring the water to a boil and then turn it down low.

_____ Last, add some salt, pepper or butter and then serve.

_____ Put one cup of rice and one cup of water in a pot with a tight lid.

_____ Let it simmer for 20 minutes.

Makes enough for 4 people.

How to make a vegetable stir-fry

Ingredients:

1. 2 cups broccoli	4.	4 celery sticks
2. 3 carrots	5.	2 tablespoons oil
3. 3 heads of bok choy	6.	1 onion

Instructions:

_____ Fry the onions until they are clear.

_____ Chop all the vegetables into small pieces on a large cutting board.

_____ Put the oil in a large frying pan or wok.

_____ First, rinse all the vegetables in a large colander.

_____ Serve with rice.

_____ Heat the frying pan.

_____ Stir in the bok choy.

_____ Add the carrots, broccoli and celery and fry them.

Many people work in a restaurant

Write the phrases next to the pictures where they belong.

1. A sous-chef prepares the trays to take out to the restaurant.
2. A dishwasher cleans the dishes, glasses and cutlery.
3. A baker prepares pies to go in the oven.
4. The chef adds spices to the soups.
5. A sous-chef chops vegetables and meat.
6. A waitress serves tables.

A.

B.

C.

D.

E.

F.

Long and Short Vowels

Long vowels sound the way we say the alphabet **A E I O U**. Short vowels are the other pronunciation. Listen to your teacher say the words and put them in the long and short vowel categories:

plate	pan	can	snack	cake
bake	stand	grate	wash	heat
tea	peel	bean	steam	cheese
slice	lid	wipe	lime	mix
slice	fish	pot	stove	chop
food	wok	spoon	cut	fry

Long	Short

Kitchen Tools - Bingo Cards

 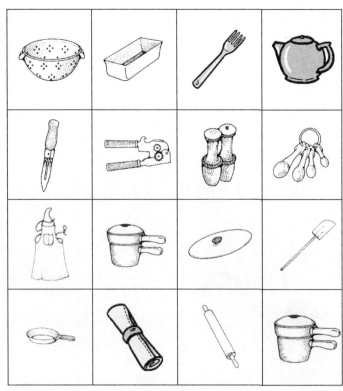

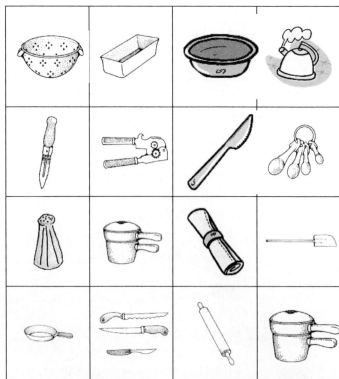

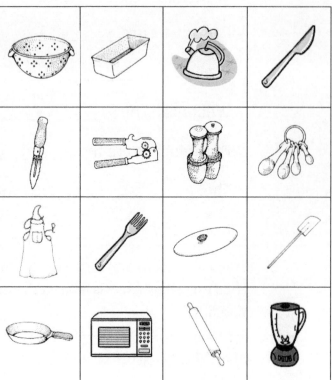

107

Kitchen Tools - Flashcards

Practise the following phrases with the flash cards with the learners:

4. Write one of the phrases on the board, show the students the pictures one at a time and the learners must say the phrase with the word.

   Could you please pass the_____?

   Do you have a_____?

   May I borrow your _____?

   Where is the _____?

   Do you know where the _____ is?

   Practise the prepositions in, on, under, beside/next to, over , and in using two images at a time and asking – Where is the_____?

   The _____ is broken.

   Can you fix my _____?

   I need a new _____.

   Where can I buy a _____?

   How much is/are the _____?

   The _____ costs $29.95. (Do this as a dictation for practising prices)

   How many _____ do you have?

5. Break the students into small groups. Give the students a set of 3-4 pictures. They must write a recipe using the items. Have them share the recipe with the class. The recipe can be made up or unusual.

6. Make a grid across the board with A B and C across the top. Put three pictures across under each letter. Add several rows to this and do a dictation either with single words, full sentences or questions.

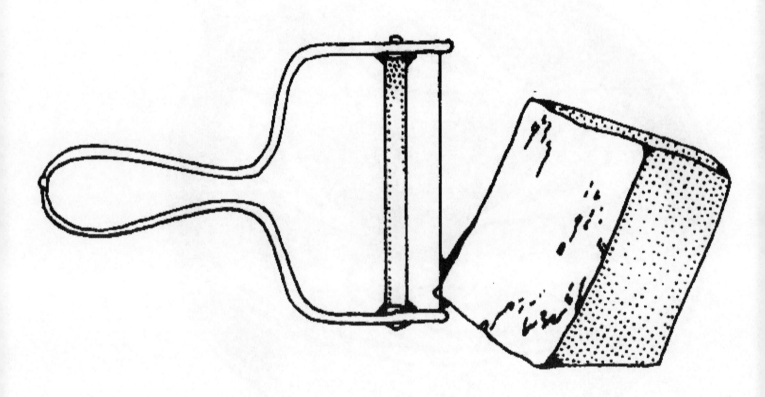

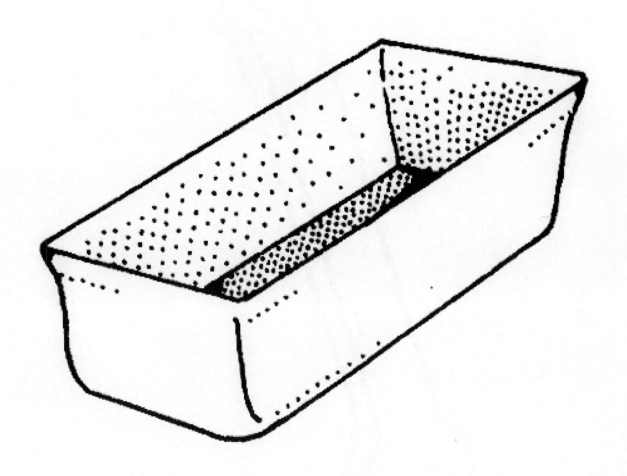

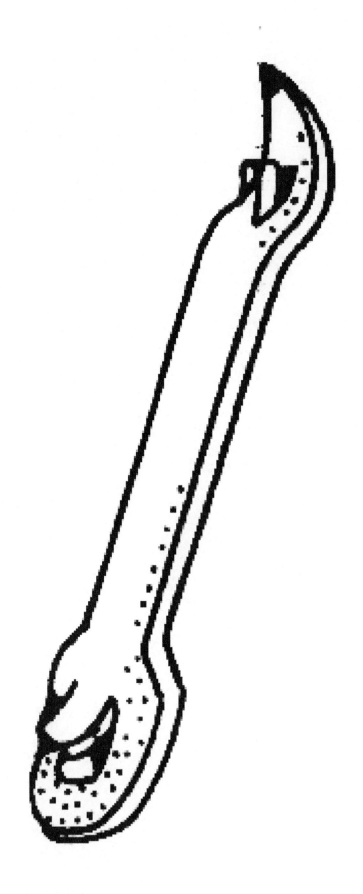

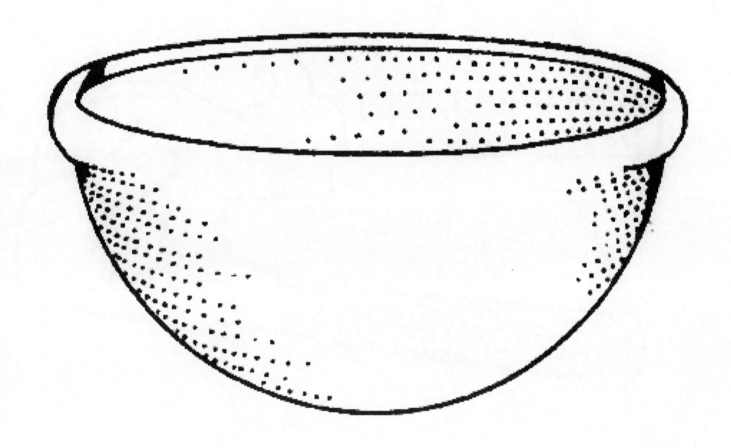

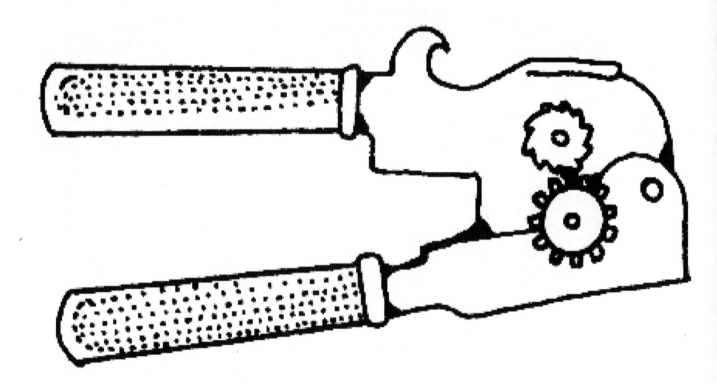

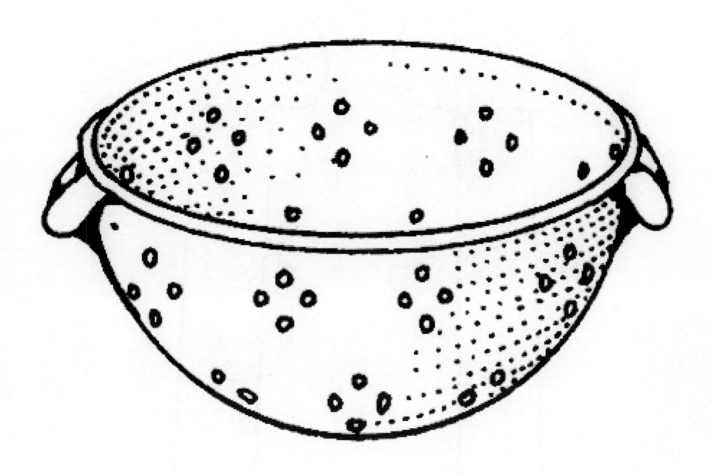

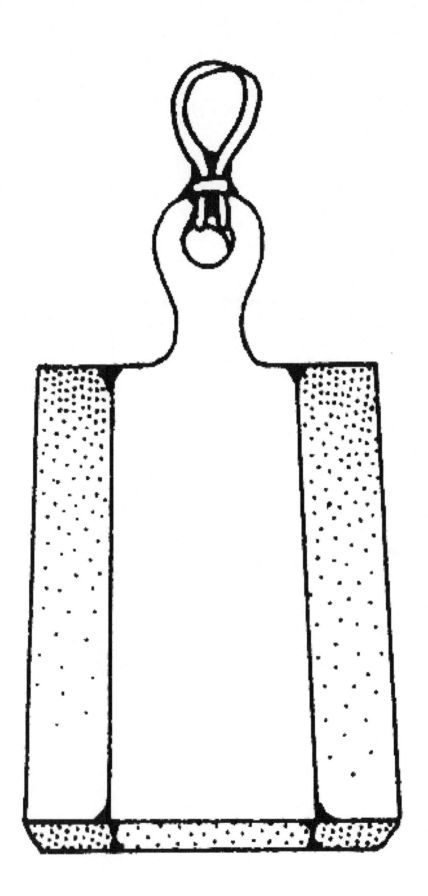

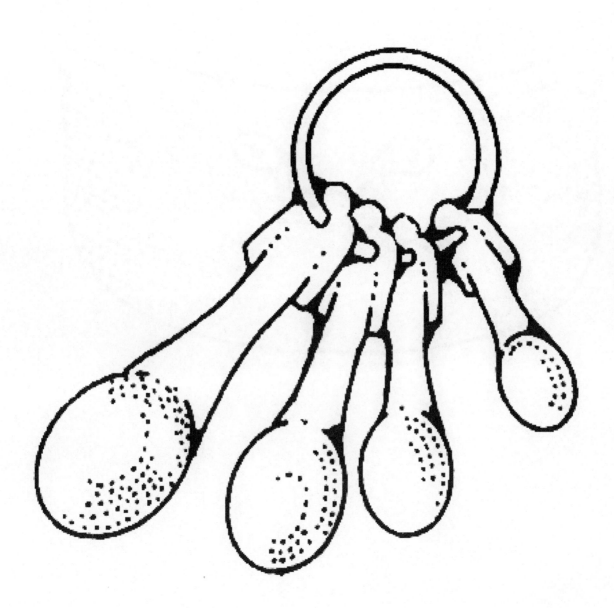

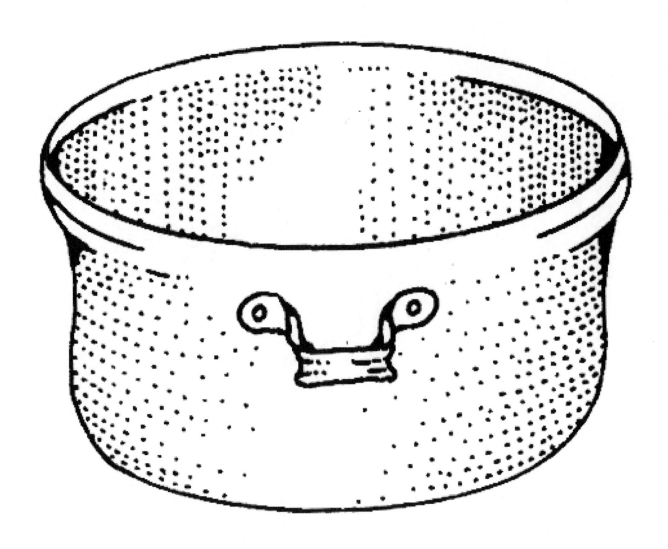

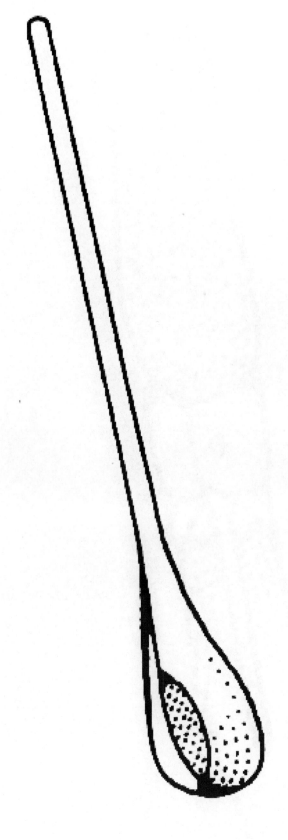

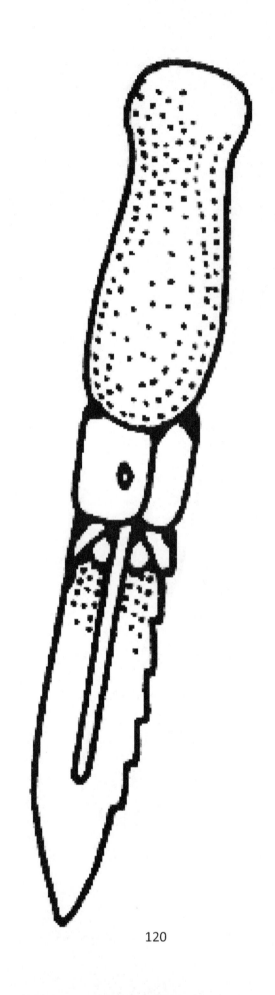

120

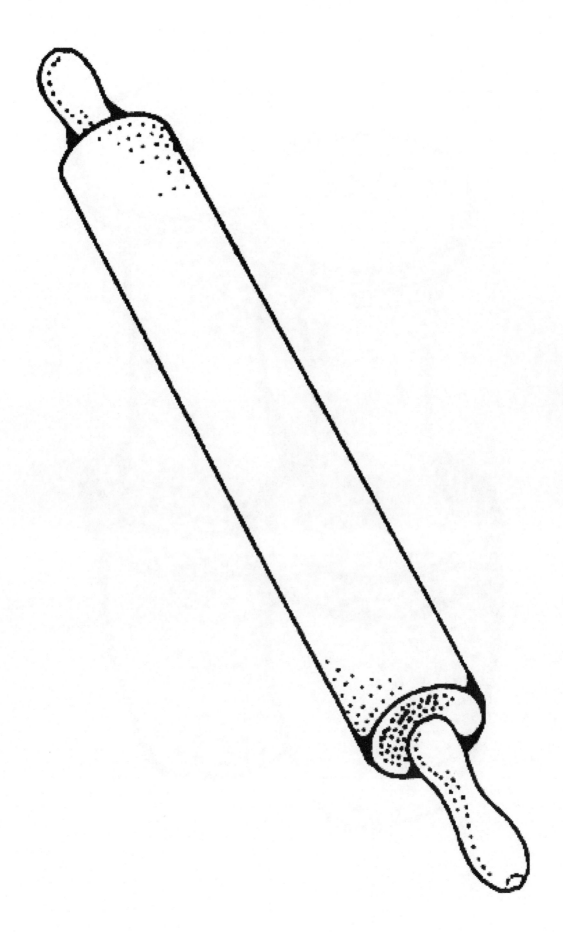

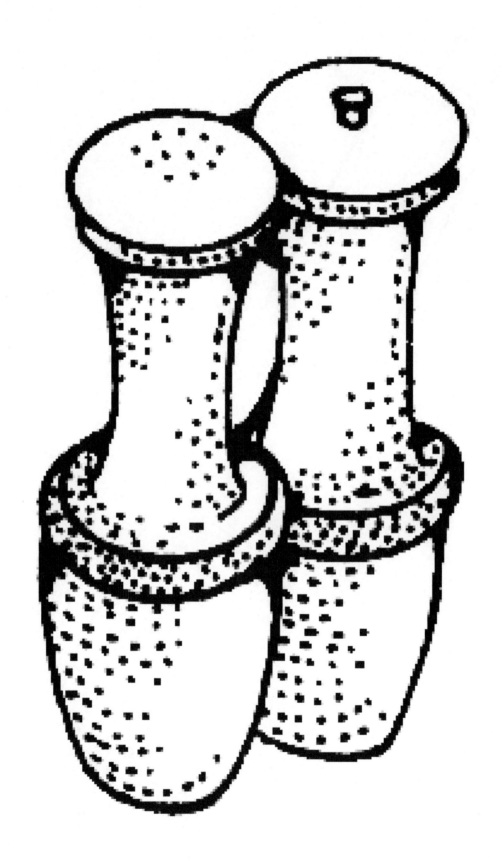

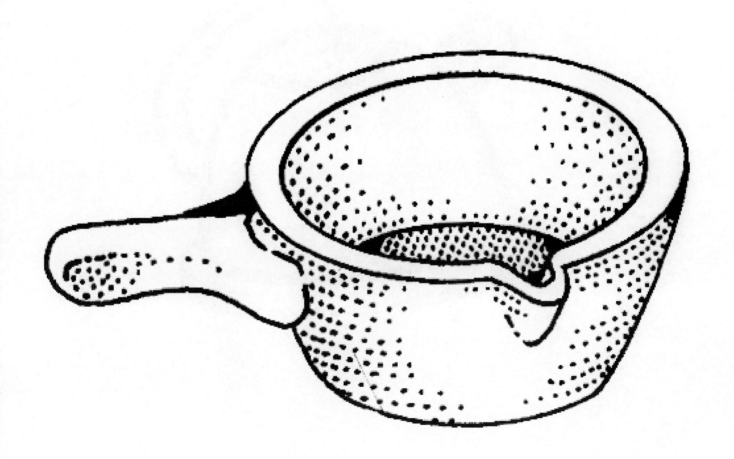

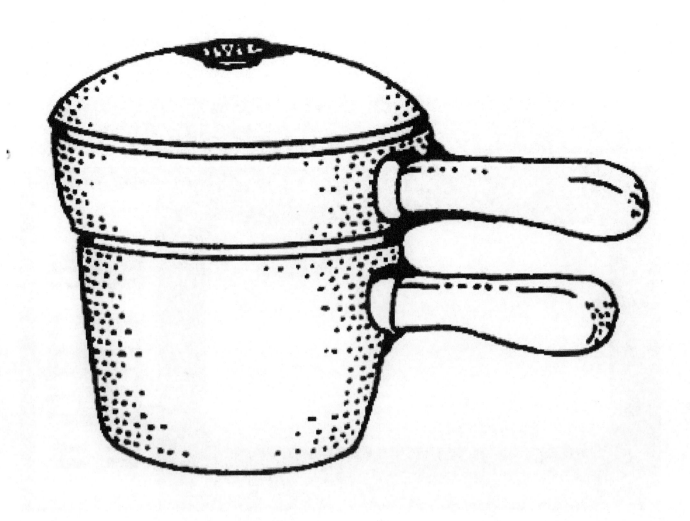

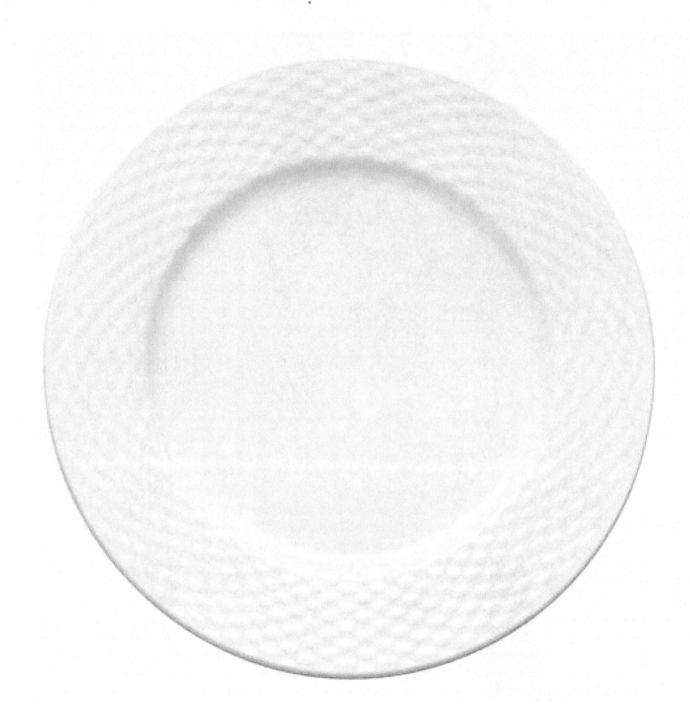

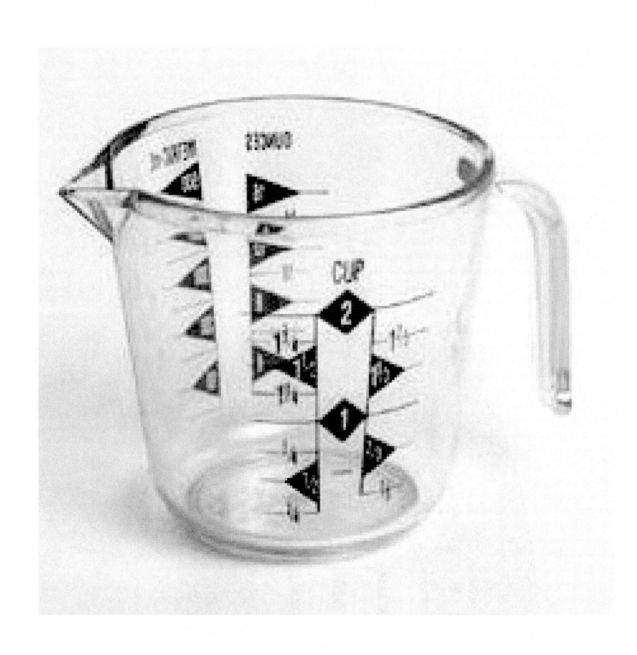

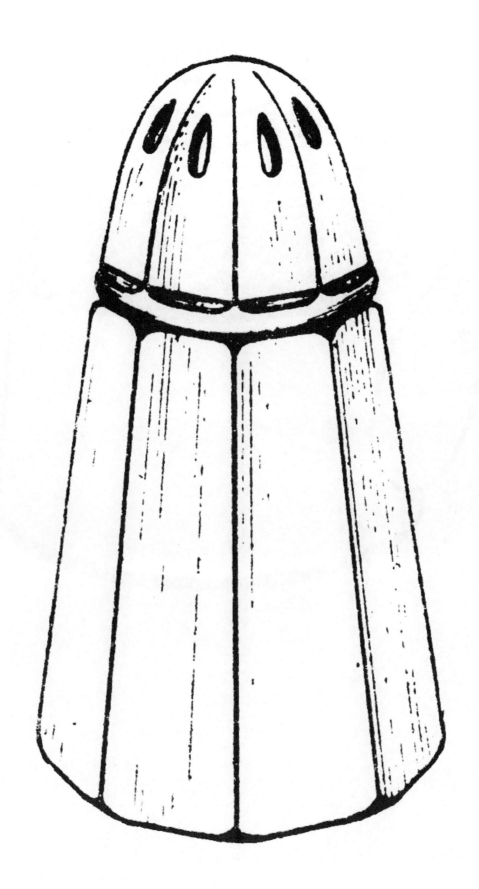

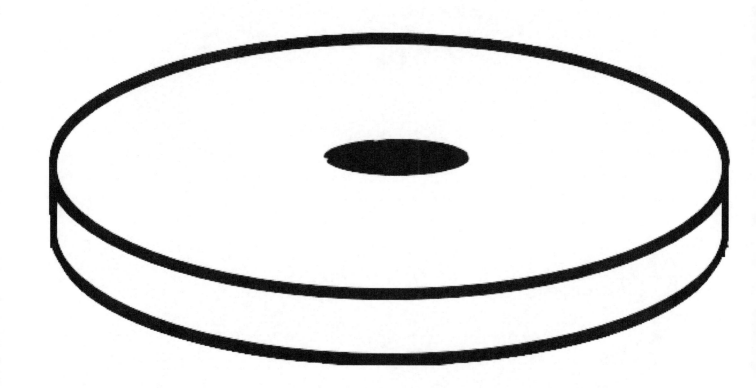

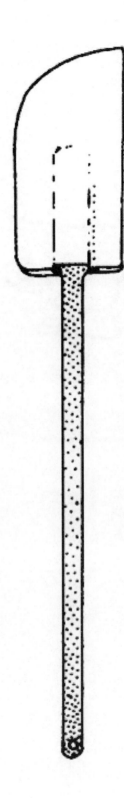

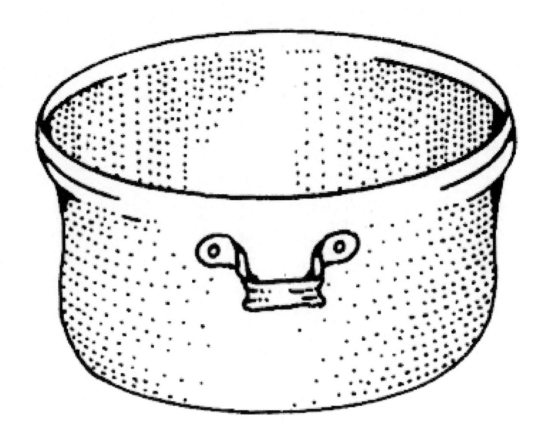

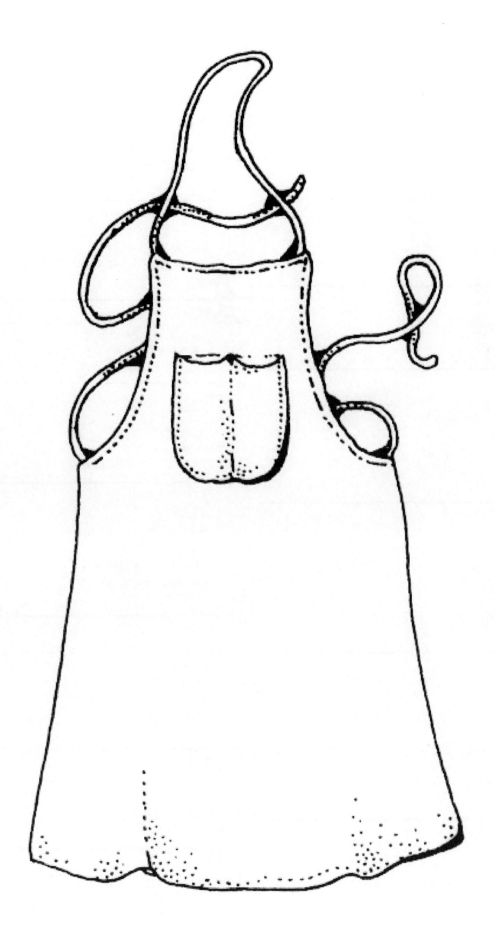

Index